T0132091

AuthorHouse™ UK
1663 Liberty Drive
Bloomington, IN 47403 USA
www.authorhouse.co.uk
Phone: 0800.197.4150

Published by AuthorHouse 03/29/2019

ISBN: 978-1-7283-8683-6 (sc)
ISBN: 978-1-7283-8682-9 (e)

Print information available on the last page.

This book is printed on acid-free paper.

authorHOUSE®

Kezzle the Lab

....

Jessica Farrington

I dedicate this book to my daughter, thank you xx
Special thanks to Sean Farrington for the illustrations xx

Kezzle is a Golden Labrador. She had two blonde lines behind her shoulder which were called her tiger stripes. Kezzle had a very playful but mischievous nature.

On her first day with her family her cheeky Nanny chased her behind the sofa with the Hoover! It took Mummy ages to get her to come out again.

Poor Kezzle

Kezzle loved a cup of tea. In her bowl was fine, but she loved it from a cup best!

Kezzle would sit on the sofa with her family as they drank tea. They would often look down to find Kezzle's head in their cup lapping up their drink!

Cheeky Kezzle

As a puppy her family often found her napping with her head in their trainers. The smellier the trainer the more she liked to nap in it.

Yucky Kezzle

Nanny went to sunbath in the garden one day. Placing A blanket and the last muffin on the grass she went to get a drink. Returning to her spot she was met with a very happy Kezzle trotting down the path with Nanny's muffin in her mouth!

Naughty Kezzle

Kezzle loved her walkies. Of an evening she would often lie on the bed with Granddad and would nudge his keys closer to him so he would take her for her walk

Clever Kezzle

On one such walk in the field, Kezzle saw some cows. Kezzle loved cows! She loved to chase them around the place. The cows didn't like this very much and they chased her instead. Kezzle doesn't like cows anymore.

Silly Kezzle

Kezzle had a favourite seat she liked to sit in. It was also her Mummy's favourite seat too. Just as Mummy was walking through the door she would jump on her Mummy's seat and lay down. Mummy had to sit somewhere else.

Sneaky Kezzle

Kezzle loved Birthdays and Christmas. Kezzle also got presents. She would open her own presents by gently ripping at the paper to get to the gifts inside.

Happy Kezzle

Kezzle sometimes liked to play Mummy and baby with her soft toys. She would lick them clean, make a nest and put them to bed all cosy and safe. Unfortunately she wasn't very good as she often trod on them and sat on their heads!

Bless Kezzle

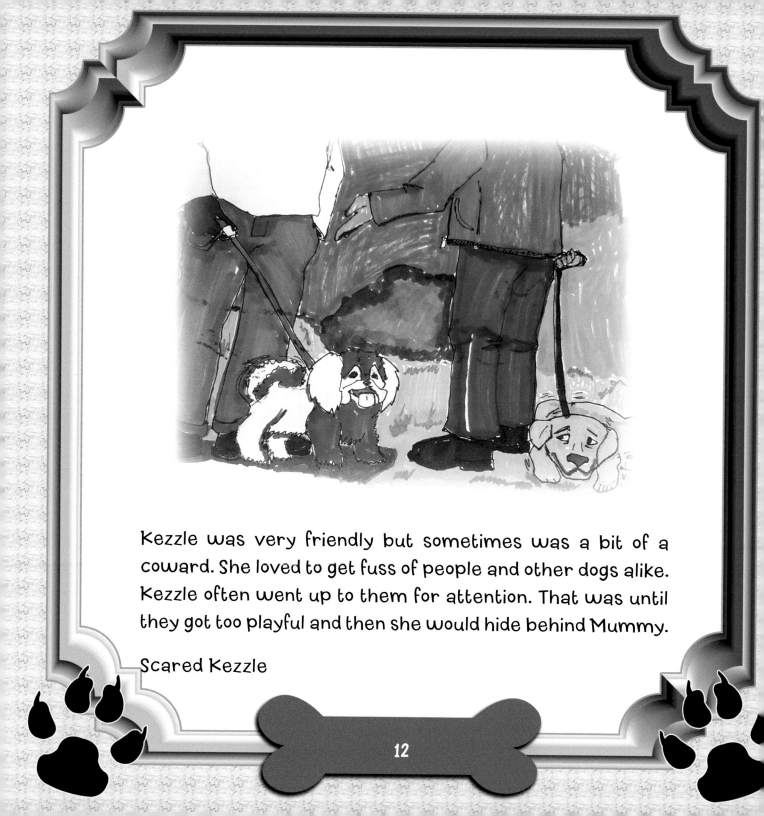

Kezzle was very friendly but sometimes was a bit of a coward. She loved to get fuss of people and other dogs alike. Kezzle often went up to them for attention. That was until they got too playful and then she would hide behind Mummy.

Scared Kezzle

Kezzle loved fuss so much if someone else was getting a fuss, she would nudge her family. If that didn't work she would just jump on them until they fussed her instead.

Jealous Kezzle

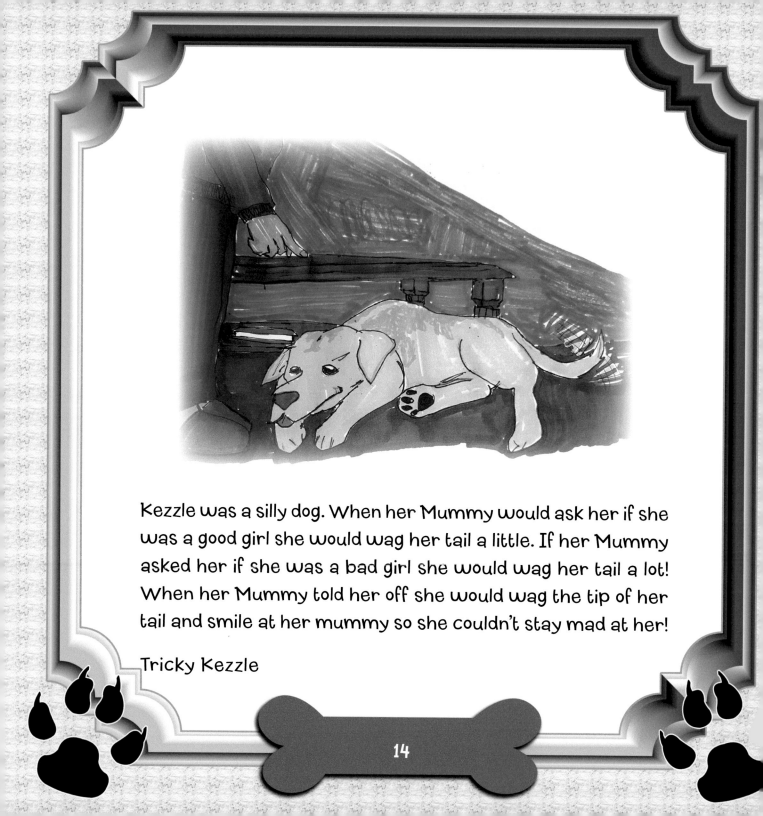

Kezzle was a silly dog. When her Mummy would ask her if she was a good girl she would wag her tail a little. If her Mummy asked her if she was a bad girl she would wag her tail a lot! When her Mummy told her off she would wag the tip of her tail and smile at her mummy so she couldn't stay mad at her!

Tricky Kezzle

Kezzle loved lying on her Mummy's bed. She would often start curled up next to her Mummy. Then very slowly she would move and start to stretch pushing her Mummy closer and closer to the edge until she pushed her mummy off the bed completely! So Kezzle would get the bed to herself

Happy Kezzle

One cold day Kezzle didn't fancy walkies. So when she and Granddad left to go to the park, she barely got out the garden when she turned round and came back home. Granddad realising she was gone came rushing back only to find her waiting for him, expecting her after walkies treat!

Naughty Kezzle

Kezzle loved her family and they loved her. Granddad was for walks and sleeping on. Nanny was for play and treats. Mummy was for food and fuss. Kezzle had them wrapped around her little paw, and they wouldn't have it any other way

Lovely Kezzle

Printed in the United States
By Bookmasters